D1085874

Holiday
SHOTS

Christmas Concoctions that Will Really Get You in the Holiday Spirit

Lindsay Herman and Devorah Lev-Tov

CIDER MILL PRESS
BOOK PUBLISHERS

13-Digit ISBN: 978-1604332414
10-Digit ISBN: 1604332417

This book may be ordered by mail from the publisher. Please include $3.75 for postage and handling.
Please support your local bookseller first!

Books published by Cider Mill Press Book Publishers are available at special discounts for bulk purchases in the United States by corporations, institutions, and other organizations. For more information, please contact the publisher.

Cider Mill Press Book Publishers
"Where good books are ready for press"
12 Port Farm Road
Kennebunkport, Maine 04046

Visit us on the Web!
www.cidermillpress.com

Design by Melissa Gerber
Photography: Steve Mann of Black Box Photography/Art direction Chris Bower
All illustrations and certain photography courtesy of Shutterstock.

Typography: Din Condensed, Savoye, Archive Kludksy, Savoire Faire,
Printed in China

1 2 3 4 5 6 7 8 9 0
First Edition

Contents

Introduction

It's that time of year again: Temperatures are dropping, sweaters are being lugged up from the basement, and the mall is a nightmare. Yup, it's the holiday season. For many people, this is a time to be with family, eat homemade food, and wrap and unwrap presents. For others, it's also a time to get wasted. After all, having a drink in hand is the only way to survive the shopping insanity, dinners for forty, and uncomfortable exchanges with Uncle Ralph.

Enter *Holiday Shots*. This book has everything you need to survive the season and maybe even enjoy it: 80 delicious (and potent!) holiday-themed shot recipes. It's also your bible for throwing the most kick-ass holiday party your friends have ever attended. Gingerbread Jell-O Men? Check. Flaming Hot Buttered Rum? Right here. Coffee Eggnog? But of course. Plus, there are winners like Mrs. Claus's Apple Cider, Peppermint Explosion, and 'Tis the Seasontini. We've also got tons of red, green, white, and gold numbers that will impress even the grumpiest grinch. We even threw in some Hanukkah and New Year's shots to cover all the boozy bases.

The first chapter offers Sweet 'n' Spicy Shots, our favorite drinks highlighting that wonderful cold-weather combo. Think apple-cinnamon and pumpkin pie but in drink form. Yum!

Fruity Shots are next, featuring flavors like melon, pineapple, cranberry, and cherry. These sweet recipes are for that girly girl in you that likes 'em to go down easy.

And now for the non–girly girl: Iron Stomach Shots. This is our chapter full of hardcore shots that will get you hammered. Expect to see lots of tequila, absinthe, and whiskey, as well as intense mixers like Tabasco sauce. Take a deep breath before shooting any of these guys back.

Next, take the edge off in Chapter 4 with our Dessert Shots. Here you'll find tasty treats like the Peppermint Patty, Kandy Kane, and Christmas Cookie. Now's your chance to have your cake and eat it too!

Chapter 5 is where you'll go for excellent eggnog-based shots. Whether you're looking for a traditional eggnog or something a little more outside the box, this chapter will make it easy.

Continuing in the dessert-y vein, Chapter 6 is all about

Jell-O Shots. It's chock-full of awesome and easy Jell-O shot recipes, like Nutcracker Jell-O Shots with Drunk Cherries, Kandy Kane Jell-O Shots, and Hanukkah Sparklers. Don't be intimidated by the Jell-O factor, we explain everything clearly and even teach you how to make fancy layered Jell-O shots.

And finally, our last chapter is a doozy: Flaming Shots. A surefire (pun!) way to kick your party into high gear, all of the shots in this chapter can be lit on fire to create dazzling spectacles. We'll show you how to light and extinguish them safely so there's no need to have the fire department on speed dial.

Whether you're a first-time bartender or a professional mixologist, a lightweight or a hardass, this book has something for everyone. Each recipe is accompanied by icons indicating its levels of difficulty and potency—both ratings are on a scale of 1 to 3, with 1 being the easiest/tamest and 3 being the hardest/strongest. Although, after a little practice making a few of the easier shots, you should be able to make the more complicated ones with no problem. (Unfortunately, we can't say the same for your alcohol tolerance.) We also noted which drinks are Christmas-colorful, meaning they are some combination of red, green, white, and gold, so you can achieve an easy wow factor. Plus, you'll find garnish suggestions and plenty of tips and recipe variations to broaden your bar menu and give your drinks a professional touch.

When the holiday season rolls around, flip through this book, mark the drinks that catch your eye, and stock your bar for your next gathering. Whether it's you and your bro, your entire extended family, your work buddies, or everyone you've ever met, *Holiday Shots* will make sure it's the celebration of a lifetime.

Shots 101

Bar Basics

Setting up your home bar is the first step to hosting a great party. Make sure you have your cabinets stocked with the following bartending staples.

GLASSWARE

Obviously, you're going to need some shot glasses. The average glass holds between 1.5 and 2 ounces, but you'll want to pick up a variety of sizes and styles. Some recipes in this book call for tall shot glasses—particularly our layered shots and shooters, which require a little showing off (these are noted in the instructions). These glasses are often a little narrower than the regular ones, and the glass is a bit thinner, so refrain from slamming them on the bar after chugging them back. For all of the flaming shots in Chapter 7, be sure to use only heatproof shot glasses.

TOOLS FOR MEASURING AND MIXING

All the recipes in this book measure ingredients in ounces. To accurately pour these shots, you'll need at least one jigger, a double-sided measuring cup with a 1-ounce container on one side and a 2-ounce container on the other. Jiggers come in a few sizes, including ½ ounce/1 ounce and ¾ ounce/1 ½ ounces, so pick up one of each to make measuring liquids a cinch.

REGULAR OLD MEASURING SPOONS ALSO COME IN HANDY WHEN PREPARING DRINKS:

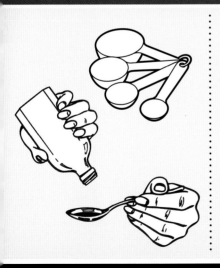

½ teaspoon = ¹⁄₁₂ ounce
1 teaspoon = ⅙ ounce
½ tablespoon = 1 ½ teaspoons = ¼ ounce
1 tablespoon = 3 teaspoons = ½ ounce
1 ½ tablespoons = 4 ½ teaspoons = ¾ ounce
2 tablespoons = 6 teaspoons = 1 ounce
3 tablespoons = 9 teaspoons = 1 ½ ounces
¼ cup = 4 tablespoons = 2 ounces
½ cup = 8 tablespoons = 4 ounces
¾ cup = 12 tablespoons = 6 ounces
1 cup = 16 tablespoons = 8 ounces

OTHER HANDY BARTENDING TOOLS

Bar spoon. This long-handled spoon makes mixing drinks easy. You can also use it when making layered shots by pouring each ingredient over the back of the spoon so it pours smoothly onto the previous layer (see pages 22 and 23 for more on layering).

Blender. If you want to make margaritas or other frozen drinks, you'll need a blender. You can find one in any kitchen supply or department store, and they range in price from $20 to $450. Don't worry, the $20 blender should be fine for these purposes. Just make sure it can blend ice.

Cocktail shaker and strainer. This beauty is essential in making any shaken drink. It looks like a large cup with a knobbed lid; it is often stainless steel. The lid comes off and there is usually a strainer at the top. All you have to do is fill it, shake it, and strain it! Pour your alcohol, mixers, and ice into the cup, cover it and shake until the ingredients blend completely, and then strain the liquid into a glass without letting any ice get into your drink to water it down. If your cocktail shaker doesn't come with a strainer, you can buy one separately.

Ice bucket and scoop. Just what it sounds like. When you're making a lot of shaken drinks, it's easiest to set up a large bucket or container of ice with a scoop so you can get to the ice quickly.

Knife and cutting board. This will come in handy for your various fruit garnishes.

Pitcher. If you're making a batch recipe (explained on page 25), you may want to set out a large pitcher of the stuff with some glasses next to it so your guests can serve themselves.

Stirrers. An easy way to class up a party, having some stirrers on hand will make mixing up your drinks simple and fun. Much cooler than a regular clumsy old spoon!

Straws. While not necessary for most shots, straws can be used to suck down a few flaming shots in Chapter 7—follow the instructions and fire-safety tips carefully. Also, if you're making other drinks that are best sipped through a straw, like mojitos or screwdrivers, your guests will thank you.

LIQUORS AND INGREDIENTS

A stocked bar should at least have the basics: beer, wine, vodka, rum, brandies, whiskey, gin, fruit juices, mixers, sodas, and some garnishes such as lemon wedges, sugar, and maraschino cherries. It's also important to have plenty of ice on hand for shaken or frozen drinks. Double check each shot recipe on your menu to make sure you have all the ingredients required.

Liquors	Popular Brands
Brandy (cognac, apple, apricot, blackberry, ginger, pear, raspberry, spiced)	Applejack, Calvados (apple), Mohawk (ginger), Hennessy (cognac)
Gin	Beefeater's, Bombay Sapphire, Gordon's, Pimm's, Seagram's, Tanqueray, Hendrick's
Rum (light, dark, overproof)	Bacardi, Captain Morgan Spiced Rum, Myers's Rum, Appleton Estate
Tequila	Jose Cuervo, Patron
Vodka	Absolut, Belvedere, Grey Goose, Ketel One, Stolichnaya, Van Gogh, Smirnoff, Skyy, Three Olives
Whiskey (bourbon, Scotch, Irish, rye)	Bushmills (Irish), Cutty Sark (Scotch), Dewar's (Scotch), Glenfiddich (Scotch), Jack Daniel's, Jim Beam (bourbon), Johnnie Walker (Scotch), Knob Creek (bourbon), Wild Turkey (bourbon), Jameson (Irish)

LIQUEURS

Advocaat (cream)

After Shock (cinnamon)

Amaretto (almond)

Anisette (anise)

Bailey's Irish Cream (cream and whiskey)

Blue Curaçao (orange)

Chambord (black raspberry)

Cointreau (orange)

Crème de Banana (banana)

Crème de Cacao (chocolate)

Crème de Menthe (mint)

Frangelico (hazelnut)

Green Chartreuse (herbal)

Godiva (chocolate)

Goldschläger (cinnamon)

Grand Marnier (orange)

Hot Damn (cinnamon)

Jägermeister (herbal)

Kahlua (coffee)

Midori (melon)

Rumple Minze (peppermint)

Sambuca (anise)

Schnapps (apple, butterscotch, cinnamon, peach, pear, peppermint, root beer, sour apple)

Southern Comfort (fruit)

Triple Sec (orange)

LIQUEURS AND SCHNAPPSES BY FLAVOR

Flavor Needed	Liqueur or Schnapps to Buy
Almond	amaretto
Anise (licorice flavor)	anisette, sambuca
Apple	apple schnapps
Banana	creme de banana
Chocolate	crème de cacao, Godiva
Coffee	Kahlua
Cinnamon	After Shock, Goldschläger, Hot Damn
Cream	advocaat, Bailey's Irish Cream
Hazelnut	Frangelico
Herbal	Green Chartreuse, Jägermeister
Melon	Midori
Orange	blue curaçao, Cointreau, Grand Marnier, triple sec
Peach	peach schnapps
Pear	pear schnapps
Peppermint	crème de menthe, Rumple Minze, peppermint schnapps
Raspberry	Chambord

MIXERS

. . . .

cream or half-and-half

eggs (for eggnog shots, see page 110)

grenadine syrup

juices: apple, cranberry, lemon, lime, orange, pineapple

milk

Red Bull

Sodas: Sprite or 7Up, Dr Pepper, club soda

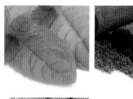

GARNISHES AND CONDIMENTS

. . . .

candy canes (mini and regular size)

cinnamon

ice

maraschino cherries

mint leaves

nutmeg

olives

pepper

peppermint candy

salt

simple syrup (see recipe below)

sprinkles

sugar (different-colored sugar can be fun around the holidays;
it's easy to find many colors in the baking aisle)

Tabasco sauce

whipped cream

Simple Syrup How-To

Simple syrup is easy to make and a great thing to have on hand if you'll be making a lot of drinks.
Just combine 1 part water with 1 part sugar in a saucepan and bring to a boil. Then lower the
heat and stir until the sugar dissolves. You can store it in a jar in the refrigerator and pull it out
whenever necessary.

 +  +

Color Makes All the Difference

Sometimes the easiest way to make something holiday-appropriate is by using seasonal colors. Many of the drinks in this book are suitable for the holidays because they are red, green, white, gold, blue, or a combination of those colors. Red, green, white, and gold work for Christmas; blue, white, and gold are perfect Hanukkah colors; and gold will remind everyone it's New Year's. In case you want to experiment with your own colorful concoctions, here's a list of relevant-colored alcohol and mixers:

Red: Chambord or other raspberry liqueur, raspberry cordial, Hiram Walker or Bols Crème de Noyaux, Campari, DeKuyper Red Apple Liqueur, pomegranate liqueur or schnapps, red curaçao, sloe gin, maraschino liqueur, UV Cherry Vodka, Hot Damn cinnamon schnapps, After Shock cinnamon liqueur, Wenneker Cinnamon Red, cherry brandy, red wine, grenadine syrup, cranberry juice, Red Bull

Green: Midori or other melon liqueur, Green Chartreuse, TY KU, green crème de menthe, green or sour apple liqueur, Bols Peppermint Green Liqueur, Carnivo XO Liqueur, absinthe, Cryptonic, UV Green Apple Vodka

White: white crème de cacao, white crème de menthe, milk, cream, half-and-half, egg white, sweetened condensed milk, coconut milk

Gold: Goldschläger cinnamon schnapps, Gold Rush cinnamon schnapps, Wenneker Gold Liqueur, Schönbrunner Gold Liqueur, Bols Gold Liqueur, Goldwasser, Gold Strike, Alizé Gold Passion Liqueur, Gold Flakes Supreme vodka, crème de banana

Blue: blue curaçao, Hpnotiq, Sourz Tropical Blue Liqueur, After Shock Blue Liqueur, Bols Blue Liqueur, Burnett's Ultra Blue Blue Raspberry Flavored Vodka, DeKuyper Island Blue Pucker Sweet and Sour Schnapps, Alizé Blue Liqueur, UV Blue Raspberry Vodka, Barton Blue Wave Raspberry Vodka, Mickey Finn Sour Blueberry Schnapps, Wenneker Blueberry Liqueur, Rose's Cocktail Infusions Blue Raspberry Drink Mix, blue raspberry fruit juice

Garnishes are also an easy way to add color. You can use red maraschino cherries, green mint leaves or other fresh herbs, a lime wedge, and white whipped cream, salt, or sugar. There are also many different colors of sugars, sprinkles, and candies that can easily add the right dash of color to your drink.

Types of Shots

Each recipe in this book is accompanied by an icon that indicates its pour technique—the techniques are Basic, Shaken, Layered, Bomb, or Batch. Here's a quick rundown of what to expect.

BASIC

As the name implies, all you need to do for Basic shots is pour the ingredient into the shot glass "neat," or by itself at room temperature. Easy!

SHAKEN

When a recipe calls for its ingredients to be "shaken," you combine them in a cocktail shaker with crushed ice, shake until it's cold and completely blended, and strain the liquid into a shot glass.

LAYERED

Here's where it gets a little complicated. But with the proper technique and a steady hand, you'll make colorful, professional-looking shots that'll wow your guests while getting them smashed. All layered shots should be poured starting with the heaviest liquid as your bottom layer, followed by the next heaviest, and so on. The very top layer should be the lightest ingredient on your list.

Take note of this easy layering technique to get the cleanest, prettiest layered shots.

LAYERING SHOTS STEP BY STEP

1. Before you begin, make sure your shot glass is tall enough to hold all layers.
2. Pour the heaviest ingredient into the bottom of a shot glass.
3. Use the back of a spoon to pour all subsequent layers: hold the spoon so the rounded side is face-up and the bottom tip is just inside the glass, hovering over the bottom layer.
4. Slowly pour the next layer over the back of the spoon. The slow-and-steady pour helps create an even top layer.
5. Keep your glass and your hand as still and steady as possible so the layers don't shift and cave in.

Liqueurs by Weight

All our ingredients are listed in the order in which they should be poured, but if you're up for experimenting with layers, keep this cheat sheet on hand to make sure yours stay put. This list ranges from heaviest (the bottom layer) to lightest (the top).

Note: Densities might vary depending on the brand. Experiment with layering beforehand if you want pitch-perfect presentation.

Grenadine syrup
Crème de cassis
Anisette
Kahlua
Crème de banana
Coffee liqueur
Green crème de menthe
White crème de menthe
Blue curaçao
Galliano (herbal liqueur)

Blackberry liqueur
Amaretto
Triple sec
Apricot liqueur
Drambuie (herbal liqueur)
Frangelico
Apricot brandy
Sambuca
Blackberry brandy
Campari (bitters)

Midori
Cointreau
Peppermint schnapps
Kümmel (herbal liqueur)
Peach schnapps
Sloe gin
Brandy
Green Chartreuse
Southern Comfort

BOMB

Bomb shots are popular among the hard-partying crowd—often enjoyed on college campuses and in sports bars, where the energy is high and chants of "chug, chug, chug" wail over the jukebox. Needless to say, these babies will supercharge your party, get your guests wasted, and likely lead to some drunken messes. All in good fun!

A bomb is a shot of liquor dropped into a glass of beer, soda, or Red Bull. First, fill a large glass about ¾ full with the beverage of your choice. Pour your liquor into a shot glass, then drop it—shot glass and all—into the beer. Guzzle it down as your friends cheer you on.

BATCH

If you're having a big party, it might be easier to make a large batch of a drink and then pour it into individual shot glasses. Recipes for eggnog, margaritas, and Jell-O shots are best made in large batches. Obviously, these recipes have a lot more of each ingredient, so make sure you have enough of everything before getting started.

Tricks of the Trade

Coating Glass Rims with Sugar or Salt

To give your shots the tasty garnish of a sugar- or salt-coated shot glass, first dip the rim of the glass in water or in the liquor (or liqueur) used in your recipe. Shake the glass to remove any extra liquid. You can also run a lemon or lime wedge over the rim to get it adequately sticky. Then dip the rim into a saucer of sugar or salt.

Chilling Glasses

If the recipe calls for chilled shot glasses—or if you want refreshing chilled glasses for all of your shots—put the glasses in the freezer for 10 minutes or in the fridge for a half hour before serving.

Special Techniques

This book includes two special techniques chapters: Jell-O Shots and Flaming Shots. Here you'll find recipes that require a set of tools and rules all their own. Below we tell you what you might need and how to prepare to make these awesome but slightly more complex shots. Make sure you read this before attempting any of the recipes in the last two chapters.

JELL-O SHOTS

Everyone loves the jiggly stuff, so why not add some booze to it and serve the dessert you know everyone's really craving? Chapter 6 contains several tasty Jell-O shot recipes, and here are a few general tips for making them quickly and easily.

BASIC TOOLS

Small plastic cups. A package of small 1- or 2-ounce plastic cups is a great thing to have on hand when making Jell-O shots. You can usually buy them in bulk, and that way your guests can dispose of them after they shoot 'em down. Glass shots may look classy, but they are actually hard to shoot from (the Jell-O gets stuck inside the glass), so you might need to provide spoons.

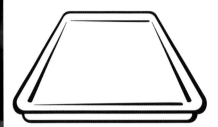

Tray or baking sheet. When you're making a large batch of Jell-O shots, it's helpful to place the small cups on a tray or baking sheet for easy and fast transference in and out of the refrigerator.

Turkey baster. This tool will help you fill your small cups easily, without drips or spills. But if you're an expert pourer, it's not essential.

Glass baking pan. If you want to try something different, instead of pouring the mixture into individual cups, pour the whole thing into a 9x13 glass baking pan. Once it sets, you can cut it into squares or use cookie cutters for fun Jell-O shapes. This works for layered Jell-O shots, too.

Cookie cutters. If you use a baking pan to make a sheet of boozy Jell-O goodness, get cookie cutters to cut out cute-shaped shots. Serve with toothpicks.

BASIC RECIPE

The basic Jell-O shot recipe involves replacing the cold water in the regular Jell-O instructions with some kind of alcohol, whether it's vodka, rum, brandy, or what have you. First, dissolve the Jell-O with hot water and wait until it's cooled to room temperature before adding the alcohol. If you add the alcohol while it's still hot, the booze will evaporate—and that's no fun for anybody. Then just follow the instructions on the Jell-O box. Ta-da!

The Awesomeness That Is Unflavored Gelatin

Unflavored gelatin is like a blank slate: It will take on the flavor of whatever you add to it, be it juice, liqueurs, or anything else you can come up with. The easiest brand to find is called Knox.

LAYER LIKE A PRO

Layered shots look impressive, and it's no different with Jell-O shots. They're a little more time-consuming than regular shots, but the effect is worth it. All you have to do is mix up each layer separately, then pour the first layer into your small cups or baking pan and let it set in the refrigerator before pouring the next, and so on. Make sure you plan ahead so you have ample time to complete these.

GARNISHES

Jell-O shots are ripe for garnishes. Whether it's whipped cream, sprinkles, crushed candy, mint leaves, or spices, garnishes can make your Jell-O shots more exciting. You can also put fruit, like a maraschino cherry, at the bottom of the cup for a fun surprise at the end of a shot.

A WORD ON ALCOHOL CONTENT

It's easy to forget that Jell-O shots actually have alcohol in them. They are colorful, taste yummy, and are fun to eat—you always want more than one. However, these shots are just that: shots. Many of them have high-proof alcohol in them such as rum or vodka, so be just as aware when you take Jell-O shots as with any other shots. If you want your Jell-O shots to be less potent, just swap out some of the alcohol for more water or mixers.

FLAMING SHOTS

With our recipes in Chapter 7, you can turn your party up to 11 with some (literal) fireworks. These shots are thrilling and beautiful when you light them up—and they taste delicious on their way down. But, remember: nothing will kill a mood like a burn injury. The risk of danger is real, so please take all the following safety precautions seriously, and serve your hot shots with care while sober. When prepared in a controlled, safe environment, flaming shots are an awesome spectacle; when prepared by idiots, someone is going to get hurt. Make sure your party is memorable for the right reasons.

YOUR BAR
. . . .
Your workspace should be clean and completely dry. Use a table, counter, or bar that's clear of tchochkes, extraneous bottles and glasses, rags, party decorations, and so on. Also remove anything nearby that's flammable, such as lampshades, chords for overhead lights, and curtains.

Last but equally important: Invest in a fire extinguisher. Please.

YOUR BOD
. . . .
Dress comfortably—and stylishly, of course—but avoid wearing loose clothing and accessories. Roll up long sleeves, tuck in baggy shirts, take off your tie, and lose the bangle bracelets.

YOUR BUDDIES

As with any fireworks exhibition, make sure spectators stand back from your workspace. Designate one responsible party guest as Fire Marshal—give him a badge to make it official but fun. As the party gets going and guests get more inebriated, you'll be thankful to have one mostly sober individual to regulate fire safety.

YOUR BOOZE

Each flaming shot recipe contains one type of liquor that is your flaming agent—usually 151-proof rum or Everclear. The super-high alcohol content in these liquors (around 75 percent) makes them easy to ignite. However, Everclear is illegal in some states, so plan your drink menu accordingly—or schedule a trip out of town for a pre-party liquor run.

Flaming agents must be 80 proof (40 percent alcohol) or higher to catch fire, but lower-proof liquors might still be harder to light. So, for recipes that call for whiskey or brandy as the flaming agent, warm the liquor before you light it by rinsing the glass in hot or boiling water. NEVER use more flaming agent than the amount indicated for the recipe. The more you use, the greater the size of the flame... and

the greater risk of losing your eyebrows (or worse!).

While pouring drinks, be sure to replace caps and corks on the bottles as you finish. Accidental spills i fire a raging, flaming disaster.

YOUR BLAZE

Use either a long campfire lighter or a long match to light your beverages. Or, to avoid affecting the taste of your shots (from butane lighters or burnt matches), use long bamboo skewers or chopsticks. Keep a large glass of water or large ashtray on hand to extinguish your match or skewer. Let your guests enjoy the flame for only five to ten seconds, otherwise you might burn the alcohol and taint the flavor.

To extinguish your drink, place an empty shot glass over the flame to snuff it out, or carefully blow it out. If you're lighting an entire row of shots, hold a wide strip of heavy-duty aluminum foil over the flames to smother the fire.

To avoid burns, instruct your shot drinkers to hold the shot glass from the bottom and avoid placing their lips directly on the rim of the glass. Finally, tell 'em to shoot those babies back quickly—do NOT sip.

Now that you know everything there is to know about holiday season shots, let's get on to the recipes! Bottoms up!

Chapter 1

Sweet 'n' Spicy Shots

There's something about wintertime that begs for the marriage of sweet and spicy. Apple cider, pumpkin pie spice, or cinnamon added to just about anything, the sweet and spicy combo warms you from the inside out. It's natural to extend that fusion to alcoholic drinks—that added boost of warmth from the alcohol is just what you need! Whether it's an alcoholic cider (Mrs. Claus's Apple Cider), a maple and cinnamon shooter (Maple Smooch), a sweet 'n' spicy martini ('Tis the Seasontini), or a zesty cranberry concoction (Cranberry Spice), this chapter has loads of creations to satisfy your sweet and spicy cravings.

Mrs. Claus's Apple Cider

If you need some TLC from grandma but with the helpful kick of alcohol, try this soothing version of apple cider that provides some extra comfort via a dose of spiced rum.

1 ounce spiced rum
½ ounce apple schnapps
½ ounce cinnamon schnapps

splash lemon-lime soda
mint leaves

1. Combine all ingredients except mint leaves with crushed ice in a cocktail shaker.

2. Shake until cold and well blended.

3. Strain into a shot glass.

4. Garnish with mint leaves if desired.

5. Feel the warmth of the most soothing cider you'll ever have.

STATS: Difficulty: 1   Potency: 2   Garnish: mint leaves

Maple Smooch

Instead of wasting calories on pancakes to get your maple kick, you can get a nice shot of New England spiked with some wintry cinnamon in this yummy shooter that's super easy to make.

1 ounce Goldschläger
1 ounce pure maple syrup

1. Pour the Goldschläger into a shot glass.

2. Add the maple syrup.

3. Stir to combine.

4. Savor the flavors of this fantastic shot!

Tip: Try to use pure maple syrup, not just maple-flavored syrup, for real and intense maple taste.

STATS: Difficulty: 1   Potency: 1

Elf Power

Ever wonder how Santa's elves stay up so late making toys? It might be due to this cinnamon-flavored burst of energy. There's something truly magical about gold flakes floating in a sea of red, don't you think?

½ ounce Goldschläger
½ ounce Red Bull

1. Pour Red Bull into a shot glass.

2. Add the Goldschläger.

3. Stir and watch the gold flakes swirl around like a special kind of snow.

STATS: Christmas-Colorful **Difficulty:** 1 **Potency:** 1

Apple-Cinnamon Sparkler

Apple and cinnamon go together like Jay-Z and Beyoncé, and just like that power combo, we also want our drinks to look good, don't we? Wow the crowd with this easy shot that sparkles and shines like the star atop your Christmas tree.

½ ounce apple vodka
½ ounce Goldschläger

1. Pour the apple vodka into a shot glass.

2. Add the Goldschläger.

3. Stir to combine and enjoy the sparkly view.

Tip: Smirnoff, Van Gogh, and Stolichnaya all make apple-flavored vodkas. If you want to add some more Christmas cheer, you can use UV Green Apple Vodka, which is—you guessed it—green.

Variation: Replace the apple vodka with Absolut's Brooklyn Limited Edition vodka, which features a blend of red apple and ginger. Yum!

STATS: Christmas-Colorful   **Difficulty:** 1   **Potency:** 2

Starry Night

Don't you just love the look of a clear, dark sky filled with stars on a cold winter's night? Recreate that imagery with the Starry Night, with the added bonus of being able to dunk a shot inside a Red Bull—aren't the holidays great?

½ can Red Bull
½ ounce Jägermeister
½ ounce Goldschläger

1. Pour the Red Bull into a large beer glass.

2. Combine the Jägermeister and Goldschläger in a shot glass—isn't it pretty?

3. Now drop the shot glass into the glass of Red Bull and chug the whole thing down!

STATS: Christmas-Colorful   **Difficulty:** 2   **Potency:** 2

Cranberry Spice

Adapted from a recipe by bartender and mixologist Dominik Chrzaszcz

Cranberries just scream Christmas, don't they? This shaken number will highlight those tart fruits and get a nice kick of ginger from the Domaine de Canton ginger liqueur. Perfect for sitting by the fireplace with your honey.

¼ ounce Chambord
½ ounce Domaine de Canton
¼ ounce cabernet sauvignon wine

1 ounce cranberry juice
2 fresh cranberries

1. Combine all ingredients except cranberries with crushed ice in a cocktail shaker.

2. Shake until cold and well blended.

3. Strain into a shot glass.

4. Garnish with cranberries if desired.

5. Try not to pucker too much from the tartness!

STATS:

Christmas-Colorful   **Difficulty:** 1   **Potency:** 2
Garnish: fresh cranberries

Holiday Drinking Games

Drinking games are always an easy way to get people at a party loosened up, or even to take the edge off a family gathering. Here are a few of our favorites, especially for the holiday season:

Blitzed Buzzwords: This game is easy to play and you can make it appropriate for any event or holiday. Just select certain "buzzwords" that signal everyone who is playing to take a drink. Buzzwords for Christmas include "Santa," "Jingle Bells," "ho ho ho," "Rudolph," and so on. Some good ones for Hanukkah are "menorah," "latkes," "candles," "dreidel," "Maccabee," and "gelt." For New Year's, try ones like "midnight," "the ball drop," "Times Square," and "resolutions."

Cockeyed Christmas Carols: This one is great for those who love to sing. Sit in a circle and have someone sing the first line of a Christmas carol. The next person has to sing the next line, and so on, until someone messes up. And you know what happens to that person—they have to drink!

Sloshed Secret Santa: Secret Santa is a common party event, and here's a way to make it even more fun. As each person opens a gift, he has to guess who gave it to him. If the guess is wrong, time to take a shot!

Drunken Dreidel: Dreidel is a classic Hanukkah game played with a special spinning top. (These are easy to find in stores around Hanukkah time.) Each side of the top has a different Hebrew letter: *gimmel*, *hay*, *nun*, and *shin*. In a regular game of dreidel, you play with gelt (aka Hanukkah money or chocolate coins) and the letter you land on decides how much gelt you get to take from the pot. For this version, shots replace the gelt! A *gimmel* means you take two shots, a *hay* means you take one shot, a *nun* means you don't do anything, and a *shin* means you tell someone else to take two shots.

Ten Before Twelve: This game is perfect for New Year's Eve, although we're not sure if it's possible to win, and it will very likely make you extremely ill. However, if you'd like to try it, here's how you play. A few minutes before midnight, line up a row of 10 shots. Turn your television on to any countdown to midnight. When they start counting down from 10, take a shot as each number is called in the countdown. If you are able to drink all 10 shots, then you are truly a machine. We told you it was crazy!

Evergreen Pine

Maybe you couldn't get a Christmas tree this year, or maybe you just have an urge to see what a drink flavored like one would taste like. Either way, this combination should remind you of that piney goodness.

1 shot glass of dry gin
1 can of Dr Pepper

1. Pour the Dr Pepper into a large glass.

2. Drop the shot of gin into the glass of soda.

3. Smells piney, doesn't it? Now drink that sucker down!

STATS: Difficulty: 1   Potency: 2

'Tis the Seasontini

If you're trying to impress someone, a martini always works. Of course, twenty minutes later you're knackered, so the impressing has probably come to a close by then. For a holiday-time version of a martini in shot form, look no further.

½ teaspoon cinnamon water (see recipe below)
¾ ounce good quality vodka
½ ounce fresh lime juice

½ ounce fresh orange juice
⅛ ounce Grand Marnier
cinnamon

1. To make cinnamon water, take a cinnamon stick and 1 teaspoon of sugar and steep them in 1 cup of boiling water for about 30 minutes. Discard cinnamon stick.

2. Pour all ingredients except cinnamon into a cocktail shaker.

3. Shake until well blended.

4. Pour into a shot or martini glass and garnish with cinnamon if you like.

5. Look sophisticated as you shoot it down.

Tip: You can double the ingredients and serve in a martini glass if you're trying to be more mature.

STATS: Difficulty: 2 Potency: 2 Garnish: cinnamon

Rudolph's Nose

You know those Rudolph toys with the blinking red noses? This shot is kind of like that, but in drink form. It will hit your taste buds on the sweet and spicy quadrants and feel warm and toasty going down.

¾ ounce Goldschläger
¼ ounce grenadine syrup

1. Pour the Goldschläger into a shot glass.

2. Slowly add the grenadine.

3. Toss that baby back!

  Christmas-Colorful   **Difficulty:** 1   **Potency:** 1

Black Cinnafruit

This fruity shot gets a nice kick from a cinnamon liqueur. Plus, if you use Goldschläger you'll get added sparkle from the gold flakes. This is a nice, tame drink that even Grandma might enjoy, if Grandma likes to do shots.

½ ounce crème de cassis
¼ ounce cinnamon liqueur
½ ounce Midori, or other melon liqueur

1. Combine all ingredients with crushed ice in a cocktail shaker.

2. Shake until cold and well blended.

3. Strain into a shot glass.

4. Revel in the multi-layered flavors.

STATS:  Difficulty: 1   Potency: 1

Chapter 2

Fruity Shots

Sometimes you just want something sweet and easy to take down, and that's okay. The drinks in this chapter are all accented with a nice fruity flavor that everyone will enjoy—these are crowd pleasers. Who can resist the Christmas Cosmo, Caramel Apple Extravagance, and Cranapple Whiskey Sour? And if you're looking for some impressive-looking red-and-green-colored drinks, you'll find shots like Holly Jolly, Dirty Christmas Tree, and Santa's Suit, which embody the Christmas spirit by using ingredients like green Midori and red grenadine syrup or Chambord. And don't worry, we won't tell anyone that you like girly drinks.

The Twelfth Night

This is a classy shot: it's clear and pleasantly fruity—perfect for spreading the Christmas cheer and impressing the ladies. You can add a nice green garnish of a lime wedge or mint leaves to brighten it up. But no pressure—we know you like to keep things simple.

1 ounce citrus vodka
½ ounce triple sec
½ ounce white cranberry juice
fresh lime juice

splash lemon-lime soda
lime wedge
mint leaves

1. Combine vodka, triple sec, and cranberry juice with crushed ice in a cocktail shaker.

2. Shake until cold and well blended.

3. Strain into a shot glass.

4. Add two squeezes of fresh lime juice and a splash of lemon-lime soda.

5. Garnish with mint leaves.

Tip: For the citrus vodka, try Absolut Citron or Smirnoff Citrus Twist.

STATS: Difficulty: 1 Potency: 2 Garnish: lime wedge or mint leaves

Holly Jolly

This red and green layered shot is easy to make and easy to make look good. It's also easy to shoot down, with its double fruity flavors that anyone will like. Cheers!

1 ounce Chambord
1 ounce Midori, or other melon liqueur

1. Pour Chambord into a shot glass.

2. Using the back of a spoon, slowly pour a layer of Midori on top.

3. Savor the season-appropriate red and green stripes, then shoot it down and savor the sweetness.

STATS:  Christmas-Colorful   Difficulty: Potency:

Golden Delicious Slammer

The slammer is a beautiful thing: It's fun to make and fun to drink, and the taste of alcohol is obscured by all the fizz. Ta-da! Teaching your friends or party guests how to slam their shots on the table and then toss 'em back will ensure them as friends for life.

1 ounce apple schnapps
1 ounce lemon-lime soda

1. Pour the apple schnapps into a shot glass.

2. Add the lemon-lime soda.

3. Cover the top of the glass with your palm, slam the shot down on the table three times, and then chug it when it's nice and fizzy.

4. Try not to burp too loudly.

Variation: The slammer can be made with any alcohol mixed with lemon-lime soda. If you're not into fruity booze, try vodka, rum, or even tequila if you are really hardcore.

STATS: Difficulty: 1 Potency: 1

Santa's Suit

Who says Santa doesn't like to throw back a few? This bright drink with a sugared rim is in honor of the jolly fat man, so toast to him as you guzzle this one down.

sugar
½ ounce Cointreau
½ ounce Chambord
½ ounce cranberry juice

1. Coat the shot glass rim with sugar (for instructions, see page 26).

2. Combine all ingredients with crushed ice in a cocktail shaker.

3. Shake until cold and well blended.

4. Strain into a shot glass.

5. Drink up!

STATS: Christmas-Colorful **Difficulty:** 1 **Potency:** 1 **Garnish:** sugared rim

Dirty Christmas Tree

Not everyone is a perfect angel and not everyone has the perfect Christmas tree. This shot celebrates those of us who are not Martha Stewart with a sweet mixture of alcohols that evokes the tropics—you know that's where you wish you were on Christmas anyway.

½ ounce coconut rum	½ ounce pineapple juice
½ ounce Midori, or other melon liqueur	splash grenadine syrup
½ ounce sweet-and-sour mix	maraschino cherry

1. Combine all ingredients except grenadine with crushed ice in a cocktail shaker.

2. Shake until cold and well blended.

3. Strain into a shot glass.

4. Top with the grenadine.

5. Garnish with a maraschino cherry if desired.

STATS:  Christmas Colorful **Difficulty:** 2
Potency: 2 **Garnish:** maraschino cherry

Christmas Tree Swirl

This red and green shot is layered and then gets a swirl from the advocaat (a creamy liqueur made from brandy, eggs, and sugar) and raspberry cordial. Fancy, huh? But not too fancy to drink, don't worry!

¾ ounce Midori, or other melon liqueur
¼ ounce Bailey's Irish Cream
2–3 drops advocaat
1–2 drops raspberry cordial

1. Pour the Midori into a shot glass.

2. Using the back of a spoon, slowly pour a layer of Bailey's on top.

3. Add the drops of advocaat and raspberry cordial and watch them sink.

4. Drink up!

STATS: Christmas-Colorful   Difficulty: 2   Potency: 2

Auld Lang Shooter

Don't be fooled by the fruity booze in this recipe. Auld acquaintances will surely be forgotten after shooting back a few of these. And isn't that just what you want after a kick-ass party?

½ ounce champagne, chilled
½ ounce Cointreau
½ ounce brandy
½ ounce carbonated water, chilled

1. Combine all ingredients in a cocktail shaker and shake until well blended.

2. Pour into a tall shot glass, and shoot!

Variation: For a smack of citrus, swap the carbonated water for ½ ounce thawed lemonade concentrate.

STATS:　　Difficulty: 1　Potency: 2

Cranapple Whiskey Sour

Cranberries and apples are a great combination in pies and juices, so obviously adding alcohol—namely, whiskey—to that mixture will only make things better. This version uses sour apple schnapps for that extra mouth-puckering punch you know you love.

⅓ ounce DeKuyper Sour Apple Pucker Schnapps
⅓ ounce whiskey
⅓ ounce cranberry juice
splash lemon-lime soda

1. Combine all ingredients with crushed ice in a cocktail shaker.

2. Shake until cold and well blended.

3. Strain into a shot glass.

4. Add a splash of soda and toss it back.

STATS: Difficulty: 1   Potency: 2

Caramel Apple Extravagance

You deserve a treat every once in a while, and surely the holiday season is that time. This shot will remind you of gooey caramel-covered juicy apples—one of life's great pleasures.

1 ounce butterscotch schnapps
1 ounce apple schnapps

1. Combine the ingredients with crushed ice in a cocktail shaker.

2. Shake until cold and well blended.

3. Strain into a shot glass.

4. Knock it back and try to resist having another. Or not.

STATS: Difficulty: Potency:

Christmas Cosmo

Ladies love cosmos, and dudes love ladies, so you should probably know how to make this drink if you're a dude. And if you're a lady, then you should definitely know how to make this drink so you can kick back and relax with this seasonal cosmopolitan.

1 ounce vodka
½ ounce Cointreau
½ ounce cranberry juice
a few squeezes of fresh lime juice
frozen or fresh cranberries

1. Combine all liquid ingredients with crushed ice in a cocktail shaker.

2. Shake until cold and well blended.

3. Strain into a shot or martini glass.

4. Garnish with one or two cranberries if desired.

5. Watch your sophistication increase as you drink up.

STATS: Difficulty: Potency: Garnish: cranberries

Partridge in a Snowy Pear Tree

This white and creamy shot looks like snow in a glass but has a nice shot of pear schnapps in it to give you that seasonal fruity kick. Sprinkle some cinnamon on top for the perfect drink.

1 ounce pear schnapps
½ ounce heavy cream
cinnamon

1. Combine the pear schnapps and heavy cream with crushed ice in a cocktail shaker.

2. Shake until cold and well blended.

3. Strain into a chilled shot glass.

4. Sprinkle cinnamon on top and enjoy!

Tip: Watching your waistline? Use half-and-half instead of heavy cream.

Variation: Instead of sprinkling the cinnamon on top you can wet the rim of the shot glass first and dip it into the cinnamon for a decorative look.

STATS: Difficulty: 1   Potency: 1

Holiday Drinking Quotes

You might think you're very clever, but instead of racking your brain for something brilliant and hilarious to say at your next holiday party, why don't you try out these funny and fitting quotes?

"The proper behavior all through the holiday season is to be drunk. This drunkenness culminates on New Year's Eve, when you get so drunk you kiss the person you're married to."

—P. J. O'Rourke

＋＋＋

"The Bible's full of wine. God ain't got nothing against a little drink to celebrate His Son's birthday with."

—Archie Bunker, on the television show *All in the Family*

＋＋＋

"Christmas at my house is always at least six or seven times more pleasant than anywhere else. We start drinking early. And while everyone else is seeing only one Santa Claus, we'll be seeing six or seven."

—W. C. Fields

＋＋＋

"What I don't like about office Christmas parties is looking for a job the next day."

—Phyllis Diller

"In the old days, it was not called the Holiday Season; the Christians called it 'Christmas' and went to church; the Jews called it 'Hanukkah' and went to synagogue; the atheists went to parties and drank. People passing each other on the street would say 'Merry Christmas!' or 'Happy Hanukkah!' or (to the atheists) 'Look out for the wall!'"

—Dave Barry

+ +

"Christmas is awesome. First of all you get to spend time with people you love. Secondly, you can get drunk and no one can say anything. Third, you give presents. What's better than giving presents? And fourth, getting presents. So four things. Not bad for one day. It's really the greatest day of all time."

—Michael Scott, on the television show *The Office*

+ +

"Oh this lovely, lovely Chanukah. So drink your gin and tonicah. And smoke your marijuanikah. If you really, really wannakah. Have a happy, happy, happy, happy Chanukah. Happy Chanukah"

—Adam Sandler

New Year's Day Mimosa

Serves 18

Whether you hit the sack pre-countdown or raged through sunrise, this morning-after shot is a light and sweet eye opener. It might even help with that hangover headache—or at least prolong the party until January 2.

½ cup Grand Marnier, or other orange liqueur
sugar
1 (750-ml) bottle chilled Brut Champagne
1 cup freshly squeezed orange juice

1. Pour ¼ cup of the Grand Marnier into a bowl, and pour the sugar into a saucer.

2. Wet the rims of all shot glasses with the Grand Marnier, then dip them in the sugar to coat them.

3. Combine the remaining Grand Marnier, champagne, and orange juice in a pitcher.

4. Pour the punch into the shot glasses, toast to your health, and toss this yummy baby back.

Chapter 3

Iron Stomach Shots

So, you fancy yourself a hardass, do you? Well, try a few of these drinks and then get back to us. The shots in this chapter have either high alcohol contents (Three Wise Men, Christmas Miracle), extreme flavors (Cinnamint Candy Cane), or both (Christmas Lights). Maybe you want to escape your family at holiday time or you're throwing the biggest, baddest holiday party ever, or maybe you just need a kick in the pants. Go ahead and mix up a few of these, but don't say we didn't warn you.

Christmas Miracle

Just to warn you, another name for this drink is Dead Man Walking. Yeah. But this green and gold sparkler will keep you in the holiday spirit and maybe even temporarily convince you that you love your annoying cousin Bernie. A true Christmas miracle.

1 ounce Goldschläger
1 ounce absinthe

1. Pour the Goldschläger into a shot glass.

2. Add the absinthe.

3. Drink with abandon.

STATS: Christmas Colorful   **Difficulty:** 1   **Potency:** 3

Snowshoe

A classic shot combining premium bourbon with peppermint schnapps—just what the doctor ordered on a cold winter's day. Let the bourbon warm you while the peppermint schnapps adds a refreshing kick.

¾ ounce peppermint schnapps
¾ ounce Wild Turkey bourbon

1. Combine ingredients with crushed ice in a cocktail shaker.

2. Shake until cold and well blended.

3. Strain into a shot glass.

4. Bottoms up!

STATS: Difficulty: Potency:

Cinnamint Candy Cane

With a double dose of sinus-clearing schnappses, this cinnamon-peppermint shot has no mixer and will definitely burn on the way down. But we know you can handle it.

1 ounce peppermint schnapps
1 ounce cinnamon schnapps

1. Pour both ingredients into a shot glass.

2. Shoot it down and breathe easy.

Tip: If you want this drink to be red, use Hot Damn or After Shock Red for the cinnamon schnapps.

STATS: Difficulty: 1 Potency: 2

Iron Stomachs Still Need To Be Informed

You may think you can handle any alcohol that comes your way, but a word to the wise: These drinks are STRONG. Some are strong because of their alcohol content, but many others are only for iron stomachs because of the mixtures of flavors and/or liquors. We caution you to read the ingredients carefully, and if you decide to drink these, make sure you are in a safe place, preferably with a designated sober friend. Oh, and have fun, too.

Santa's Little Helper

How do you think Santa stays up all night? Absinthe can make any party better, and this festive red-and-green shot, also known as the Wolf Bite, definitely benefits from a nice dose of it. This shot tastes so good that your guests will definitely be asking for seconds and thirds—and that's when the fun starts.

½ ounce Midori, or other melon liqueur
½ ounce absinthe
½ ounce pineapple juice

Splash lemon-lime soda
drizzle of grenadine syrup

1. Combine Midori, absinthe, and pineapple juice with crushed ice in a cocktail shaker.

2. Shake until cold and well blended.

3. Strain into a shot glass.

4. Add a splash of lemon-lime soda and a drizzle of grenadine syrup on top.

5. Let the revelry begin!

STATS:  Christmas-Colorful   Difficulty: 2   Potency: 3

Peppermint Explosion

If the holiday season means peppermint ice cream and candy canes to you, this is your drink. The double dose of peppermint-flavored alcohols will make your throat burn, but at least your breath will be fresh.

1 ounce peppermint schnapps
1 ounce Rumple Minze peppermint liqueur
splash of cold milk

1. Combine peppermint schnapps and Rumple Minze in a shot glass.

2. Add milk.

3. Shoot it back and make your eyes tear.

Variation: If you're really hardcore, don't bother with the milk.

STATS: Difficulty: 1   Potency: 2

76

Christmas Cranberry Margarita Shots

Serves 16

This recipe is perfect if you're having a party—you can make one large batch of these cranberry margaritas and then serve them in shot glasses for a perfect holiday hors d'oeuvre.

¾ cup tequila
½ cup Grand Marnier, or other orange liqueur
1½ cups cranberry juice
¾ cup fresh lime juice

½ cup sugar
1½ cups frozen cranberries, rinsed
ice
sugar

1. Combine all liquid ingredients, sugar, and cranberries with crushed ice in a large blender.

2. Pulse for a few minutes, until well blended.

3. Coat the shot glass rims with sugar (for instructions, see page 26).

4. Pour the margarita mixture from the blender into the shot glasses.

5. Garnish with frozen cranberries if you have some leftover.

6. Watch your party go from ho-hum to awesome.

Tip: If you have a small blender, you can mix these up in batches. Just combine all the liquids and the sugar and cranberries in a large bowl or pitcher, and then pour in as much as will fit in your blender with ice and repeat until it's all blended.

STATS:
Christmas-Colorful   **Difficulty:** 2   **Potency:** 3
Garnish: cranberries, sugar rim

Lemon-Champagne Fizz

Add a little hard stuff to your New Year's party with this citrusy gin shot. Your guests won't know what hit 'em (till the next morning, anyway).

½ ounce gin
⅓ ounce lemon juice
pinch superfine sugar
1 ounce champagne, chilled
lemon wedge

1. Combine the gin, lemon juice, and sugar with crushed ice in a cocktail shaker.

2. Shake until cold and well blended.

3. Strain into a shot glass.

4. Top with champagne, and knock it back!

STATS: Difficulty: 1 Potency: 2 Garnish: lemon wedge

Christmas Lights

This shot is sure to impress your friends and guests because it looks like a red light floating in a glass. And of course, it's floating in a mixture of rum and tequila, so pretty soon they'll be seeing lights everywhere.

½ ounce rum
½ ounce tequila
4–6 drops Tabasco sauce

1. Pour the rum and tequila into a shot glass.

2. Squeeze out a few drops of Tabasco sauce into the glass.

3. Stir it up and the Tabasco should float to the middle.

4. Soak up the praise from all your friends.

STATS: Christmas-Colorful   Difficulty: 2   Potency: 3

Black Peppermint Shooter

There's nothing like a little Jäger to get a party started, am I right? Fair warning: This shot is also known as Liquid Cocaine, so be careful and don't drink too many of these in one sitting.

1 ounce Jägermeister
1 ounce peppermint schnapps

1. Pour Jägermeister into a shot glass.

2. Add the peppermint schnapps.

3. Prepare to get wasted.

Tip: Throwing back shots of Jägermeister is a surefire way to get knackered. You'll feel great after one, but after three... try to have a friend make sure you don't do anything too stupid.

STATS: Difficulty: 1 Potency: 2

Three Wise Men

No, not *those* three wise men! We're talking Jim, Jack, and Johnnie, of course! What could be more fitting for Christmas than this shot made up of your three best friends?

½ ounce Jim Bcam Bourbon
½ ounce Jack Daniel's Tennessee Whiskey
½ ounce Johnnie Walker Scotch Whisky

1. Pour all ingredients into a cocktail shaker.

2. Shake until cold and well blended.

3. Strain into a shot glass.

4. Bottoms up!

Variation: **Three Wise Men Go Hunting**: Add ½ ounce Wild Turkey Bourbon.

Variation: **Three Wise Men Visit Mexico**: Add ½ ounce Jose Cuervo Gold Tequila.

STATS: Difficulty: 1   Potency: 3

Hangover Help 101

Nothing will taint your memories of an evening of revelry like a head-splitting, bowel-purging, zombie-walking hangover. You can prevent that drill-hammer headache—and miserable hours wrapped around the toilet bowl—by following these simple rules.

1. **Eat, eat, eat!** Eat a full meal before you start drinking to create a base in your empty stomach. This will slow the alcohol's absorption into your system, keep you from getting hammered too quickly, and protect the lining of your stomach. Try to snack a bit while drinking, too. For maximum booze-absorption, munch on foods that are heavy in carbs and proteins—nuts, crackers, breads, and cheeses are all excellent snack options to have on hand.

2. **Don't mix.** If you're drinking vodka shots, stick with vodka shots. If you've already had three rum-based shots, don't down three tequila shots next. Mixing alcohols is a surefire way to end up hurting in the morning. Each type of alcohol contains its own distinct set of chemicals, and when combined, they make it more difficult for your body to metabolize the booze.

3. **Hydrate!** Alcohol is extremely dehydrating; it lowers your levels of electrolytes and your blood sugar. That's what causes the wicked headaches and dizziness after a night of drinking. To stay hydrated while partying, alternate those alcoholic beverages with glasses of water—that way, you'll stay on your toes (literally) and minimize the post-party bodily damage. Then drink a large glass of water before bed. You should also equip your fridge with sports drinks like Gatorade and fruit juice for morning-after pick-me-ups.

4. **Stay up late.** The longer you stay awake, the more time your body will have to metabolize all the alcohol you just drank.

Hangover Helpers

If it's too late and you're already aching with the effects of too much drink, toss some of this stuff down your gullet to replenish vitamins and electrolytes and flush out toxins:

- Water
- Bananas
- Fruit juice
- Sports drinks
- Eggs

Hangover Cure Myths

Beware of these frequently touted hangover remedies. Not only will they not make you feel any better, they can draw out your symptoms and even make you sicker.

Myth 1
Hair of the Dog: The age-old remedy of drinking even more booze the following day will *not* quicken your hangover recovery—it'll only prolong the detox process and continue battering your liver. Swap that brunch-time Bloody Mary for straight OJ instead.

Myth 2
Coffee: Like alcohol, caffeine is a diuretic that'll make you pee often and keep you dehydrated.

Myth 3
Fatty, greasy foods and dairy: Stay away from foods that are tough on your tummy—you've already doused it with loads of alcohol, so oils, fats, and milk products will only cause more upset.

Myth 4
Painkillers: Contrary to popular belief, over-the-counter painkillers containing acetaminophen, such as Tylenol, will *not* help prevent hangover headaches. In fact, they can do serious damage to your already-weakened liver. Stock up on ibuprofen instead.

Chapter 4

Dessert Shots

Screw the cakes, pies, puddings, and Christmas cookies. Holiday festivities don't *really* begin until you're downing something delicious *and* alcoholic. Lucky for you, in this chapter we've collected twenty delectable shot recipes that'll sate your sweet tooth while getting you drunk. What could be better? From gingerbread to oatmeal cookies and peppermint patties to tiramisu, the dessert shot menu is long, broad, and irresistible.

Nutcracker Shooter

You don't need a nutcracker to enjoy the nutty goodness of this hazelnut-almond shooter. The real star here is the Amarula Cream: a slightly sweet, creamy liqueur made from the boozy fruit of the South African malura tree.

½ ounce Frangelico
½ ounce amaretto
½ ounce Amarula Cream

1. Pour Frangelico into a shot glass.

2. Using the back of a spoon, slowly pour a layer of amaretto on top of the Frangelico.

3. Again using the spoon, layer Amarula Cream on top.

4. Enjoy this delicious, nutty shot.

STATS: Difficulty: 2   Potency: 2

Mistletoe Aperitif

Who needs an herb as an excuse to pucker up? This colorful, layered shot of mojo will help you muster the nerve to approach that cutie at your Christmas party.

½ ounce Chambord	½ ounce Grand Marnier, or other orange liqueur
½ ounce Midori, or other melon liqueur	mint leaves

1. Pour Chambord into a tall shot glass.

2. Using the back of a spoon, slowly pour a layer of Midori on top of the Chambord.

3. Again using the spoon, layer Grand Marnier on top.

4. Garnish with mint leaves if desired and gather your courage for that smooch.

STATS:  Christmas-Colorful **Difficulty:** 2 **Potency:** 2
Garnish: mint leaves

Peppermint Patty

This classic candy in a shot glass is creamy and minty—the perfect shooter for holiday soirees. Vary the portions according to your preference: if you're a chocoholic, use more crème de cacao; go heavy on the schnapps if you fancy a minty-cool flavor.

½ ounce crème de cacao
½ ounce peppermint schnapps
1 ounce cream
whipped cream

1. Combine all ingredients with crushed ice in a cocktail shaker.

2. Shake until cold and well blended.

3. Strain into a shot glass.

4. Top with whipped cream to make it even more decadent.

STATS: Difficulty: 1   Potency: 1   Garnish: whipped cream

Sweet Santa

Sweeten up the festivities with this delicious candy cane–flavored shot. The red, green, and white layers add decorative flair to an already irresistible concoction.

⅓ ounce grenadine syrup
⅓ ounce green crème de menthe
⅓ ounce peppermint schnapps

1. Pour grenadine into a shot glass.
2. Using the back of a spoon, slowly pour a layer of crème de menthe on top of the grenadine.
3. Again using the spoon, layer peppermint schnapps on top.
4. Admire this striped beauty before you chug it down.

STATS:  Christmas-Colorful   **Difficulty:** 2   **Potency:** 1

Boost Your Booze IQ

Peppermint schnapps and crème de menthe are both minty and delicious, but they're not interchangeable. The schnapps has a lighter body and higher alcohol content, so stick with the ingredient listed to get the recipe right. Try yummy peppermint schnapps by DeKuyper, Arrow, or Hiram Walker.

Kandy Kane

Replicate the season's most beloved candy with this minty red-and-white shot. The contrasting flavors—smooth almond in the Crème de Noyaux and cool peppermint in the peppermint schnapps—will bring a little sparkle to your palate.

1 ounce peppermint schnapps	red-and-white mint candy
1 ounce Crème de Noyaux	

1. Pour the peppermint schnapps into a tall shot glass.

2. Using the back of a spoon, slowly pour a layer of Crème de Noyaux on top.

3. Drop a red-and-white mint candy into the glass for a lasting minty aftertaste.

Tip #1: Make sure you use a red Crème de Noyaux for the proper Christmas colors. Hiram Walker and Bols both sell red Crème de Noyaux.

Tip #2: Warn your guests not to choke on the candy!

STATS: Christmas-Colorful **Difficulty:** 1 **Potency:** 1 **Garnish:** mint candy

Christmas Cookie

This tasty cookie is easy to make—just mix the liqueurs in a cocktail shaker, pour into a shot glass, and knock it back. Yum!

½ ounce peppermint schnapps	whipped cream
½ ounce Kahlua	maraschino cherry
½ ounce Bailey's Irish Cream	sprinkles

1. Combine all liquid ingredients with crushed ice in a cocktail shaker.

2. Shake until cold and well blended.

3. Strain into a shot glass.

4. Garnish with whipped cream, cherry, green and red sprinkles, or all three if you're feeling truly decadent.

STATS: Difficulty: 1   Potency: 2
Garnish: whipped cream, maraschino cherry, sprinkles

Oatmeal Cookie Shooter

This cookie-with-a-kick is sweet going down, but be forewarned: It's not for the weak-kneed. Pair it with raisins to help soak up the booze—stick a few on a toothpick for an oatmeal-raisin twist.

¾ ounce butterscotch schnapps
¾ ounce Dailey's Irish Cream
splash of Jägermeister

splash of cinnamon schnapps
raisins

1. Combine all ingredients except raisins with crushed ice in a cocktail shaker.

2. Shake until cold and well blended.

3. Strain into a shot glass.

4. Garnish with raisins and savor your treat.

 STATS: **Difficulty:** 2   **Potency:** 2   **Garnish:** raisins

White Snow

Vanilla, peppermint, and heavy cream join forces to make this shooter a refreshing, pure-white treat. Garnish with a mini candy cane for extra merriness.

½ ounce heavy cream
½ ounce vanilla vodka
½ ounce peppermint schnapps

½ ounce white crème de cacao
mini candy cane

1. Combine all ingredients except candy cane with crushed ice in a cocktail shaker.

2. Shake until cold and well blended.

3. Strain into a chilled shot glass.

4. Garnish with mini candy cane, if desired.

5. Revel in the minty freshness!

STATS: Difficulty: 2 Potency: 3 Garnish: mini candy cane

Snowball Smash

If you're looking for that snowball-to-the-face sting, the Snowball Smash is your drink. Don't be fooled by the mouthwatering chocolate-mint-candy ingredients—this shot will get you loaded while tickling your tongue.

½ ounce brandy
½ ounce peppermint schnapps

½ ounce white crème de cacao
whipped cream

1. Combine all ingredients with crushed ice in a cocktail shaker.

2. Shake until well blended.

3. Strain into a shot glass.

4. Garnish with whipped cream and knock it back!

Variation: For a less boozy alternative, nix the brandy and use 3/4 ounce each of Schnapps and crème de cacao instead.

STATS:　　Difficulty: 1　Potency: 2　Garnish: whipped cream

St. Nick's Spirit

The almond-flavored Crème de Noyaux gives this fruity shooter a rich finish. Spiff it up with a dollop of whipped cream or a cherry garnish—or both!

¾ ounce red Crème de Noyaux
¾ ounce red Midori
whipped cream
maraschino cherry

1. Pour the Crème de Noyaux into a shot glass.

2. Using the back of a spoon, pour a layer of Midori on top.

3. Garnish with whipped cream and a stemless maraschino cherry.

4. Feel the spirit of St. Nick as you guzzle it down.

STATS: Christmas-Colorful **Difficulty:** 1 **Potency:** 2
Garnish: whipped cream, maraschino cherry

O Christmas Tree

We're not saying you have to belt out a drunken rendition of "O Tannenbaum" while you chug this shot, but it will certainly kick your party into high gear. Top the tree with whipped cream or a cherry for a sweet garnish.

⅓ ounce green crème de menthe
⅓ ounce grenadine syrup
⅓ ounce Bailey's Irish Cream
whipped cream
maraschino cherry

1. Pour crème de menthe into a shot glass.

2. Using the back of a spoon, slowly pour a layer of grenadine on top of the crème de menthe.

3. Again using the spoon, layer the Bailey's on top.

STATS:  Christmas-Colorful   **Difficulty:** 2   **Potency:** 1
Garnish: whipped cream, maraschino cherry

Carrot Cake

This delicious cake-in-a-glass recipe tastes just like the real thing. The best part: It doesn't have nearly as many calories as a slice of cake. But good luck trying to chug just one.

⅓ ounce Frangelico
⅓ ounce butterscotch schnapps
⅓ ounce cinnamon schnapps

1. Combine all ingredients with crushed ice in a cocktail shaker.

2. Shake until cold and well blended.

3. Strain into a shot glass.

4. Toss it back and try to resist repeating.

 STATS: Difficulty: 1   Potency: 2

Irish Christmas Coffee

If you're looking to kick the party up a notch, try this delicious coffee-flavored bomb shot. You'll need a pint glass or beer mug, plus plenty of endurance for chugging.

1 ounce Bailey's Irish Cream
1 ounce Van Gogh Double Espresso Vodka
Guinness beer, in a large glass

1. Pour the Bailey's into a shot glass.

2. Pour a layer of vodka on top.

3. Pour the Guinness into a pint glass ¾ of the way full. Let the beer settle.

4. Drop the shot glass into the Guinness, and chug it!

STATS: Difficulty: 2   Potency: 3

Gingerbread Man

For a lip-smacking Christmas treat, replicate the flavor of your favorite anthropomorphized cookie in a tall shot glass.

1 ounce Bailey's Irish Cream
½ ounce butterscotch schnapps
½ ounce cinnamon schnapps

1. Combine all ingredients with crushed ice in a cocktail shaker.

2. Shake until cold and well blended.

3. Strain into a tall shot glass.

4. Satisfy your sweet tooth.

Variation: To get an authentic spicy-sweet gingerbread flavor, look for Hiram Walker's seasonal Gingerbread Liqueur at your local liquor store. Halve the Bailey's Irish Cream and add ½ ounce Gingerbread Liqueur.

STATS: Difficulty: 1   Potency: 2

Kris Kringle

It's easy to imagine the big guy reaching for this creamy root beer–flavored shot during his sleigh-ride downtime. Similar to a root beer float, the Kringle has a slightly sweet, refreshing aftertaste.

½ ounce amaretto
½ ounce root beer schnapps
¼ ounce half-and-half
maraschino cherry

1. Combine the amaretto and root beer schnapps in a shot glass.

2. Using the back of a spoon, slowly pour a layer of half-and-half on top.

3. Garnish with a maraschino cherry and enjoy.

STATS:  **Difficulty:** 2   **Potency:** 2   **Garnish:** maraschino cherry

Tiramisu Shooter

For an Italian touch to your holiday festivities, replicate the delicious layers of tiramisu with boozy substitutions: Kahlua for the coffee, advocaat for the creamy mascarpone, and a smidge of cinnamon schnapps for a little spice.

½ ounce golden rum	1 teaspoon cinnamon schnapps
½ ounce Kahlua	whipped cream
½ ounce advocaat	maraschino cherry

1. Combine all liquid ingredients with crushed ice in a cocktail shaker.

2. Shake until cold and well blended.

3. Strain into a shot glass.

4. Garnish with whipped cream and a cherry.

5. Try to refrain from speaking with an Italian accent after more than one of these.

STATS: Difficulty: 1   Potency: 3
Garnish: whipped cream, maraschino cherry

Chocolate-Covered Cherry

Liquor-filled cherry cordials are an all-time favorite Christmas treat, and they deserve an even boozier adaptation. Herewith, the Chocolate-Covered Cherry—a sweet, cherry-tinged confection that's pretty darn close to the real thing.

½ ounce Kahlua
½ ounce amaretto
½ ounce Bailey's Irish Cream

splash grenadine syrup
maraschino cherry

1. Combine the liqueurs in a shot glass in the order listed.

2. Add a splash of grenadine on top.

3. Garnish with a stemless cherry.

STATS: Difficulty: 1   Potency: 2   Garnish: maraschino cherry

Maccabee Pride

This blue and white shot will remind you how Judah and the Maccabees saved the Jews from destruction on Hanukkah. Plus, the chocolate-orange combination is sublime.

1 ounce white crème de cacao
1 ounce blue curaçao

1. Pour the crème de cacao into a tall, chilled shot glass.

2. Using the back of a spoon, slowly pour a layer of the blue curaçao on top of the white crème de cacao.

3. Applaud your handiwork before slurping it down.

STATS:  Hannukah-Colorful   **Difficulty:** 2   **Potency:** 1

Chocolate Cake

Everyone knows it's proper to eat chocolate around the holidays. Get your chocolate cake fix with this magical little no-bake (and non-fat!) recipe. Hazelnut liqueur and citrus vodka combine to replicate the flavor of cake, while a sugar-coated lemon wedge serves as the frosting.

½ ounce Frangelico
½ ounce citrus vodka, such as Absolut Citron
sugar
lemon wedge

1. Combine Frangelico and vodka with crushed ice in a cocktail shaker.

2. Shake until cold and well blended.

3. Strain into a shot glass.

4. Coat the lemon wedge in sugar. Then lick the back of your hand and sprinkle sugar on top.

5. Shoot the liquor, lick the sugar, and suck on the lemon wedge.

STATS: Difficulty: 2   Potency: 2   Garnish: lemon wedge

Cherry Bomb

How 'bout some cherry cola with a little kick? The vodka–Red Bull combo will keep you from tuckering out on party night, while the cherry flavors make this a sweet-as-soda treat. Add the grenadine gradually, without mixing, for a floating red color effect.

½ ounce cherry vodka
1 ½ ounce Red Bull energy drink
splash grenadine syrup
maraschino cherry

1. Combine vodka and Red Bull in a shot glass.

2. Slowly pour grenadine into the glass so it sinks to the bottom.

3. Plop a cherry in the glass and toss it back.

Tip: Try Three Olives Cherry Vodka or UV Red Cherry Vodka for maximum cherry flavor.

STATS: Christmas-Colorful   **Difficulty:** 1   **Potency:** 1
Garnish: maraschino cherry

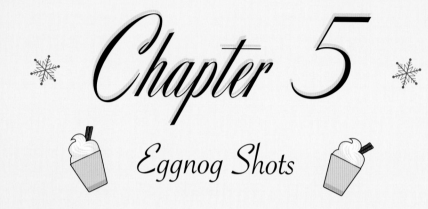

Chapter 5

Eggnog Shots

Eggnog is the quintessential holiday beverage: creamy, comforting, and—yup—alcoholic. The yummy combo of milk, sugar, raw eggs, and spices is an age-old Christmas tradition in most American families. But the basic recipe is also an international standard, with variations such as *coquito* (in Puerto Rico), *biersuppe* (in Germany), *rompope* (in Mexico), and *biblia con pisco* (in Peru).

Since homemade eggnog requires some real preparation, you'll need to make a larger batch of it for your holiday eggnog shots. Just prepare your 'nog ahead of time, then pour into shot glasses when the party calls for it. You can also make a large batch of non-boozy eggnog and only use a portion of it for shots (that way, the kiddies and designated drivers won't feel left out of the milkshake-y revelry). Either way, these creamy shots will be a deliciously festive—and festively delicious!—addition to your party.

Brandy Eggnog

Serves 4

This rum-less variation is a bit lighter than our Traditional Eggnog (on page 112), with tawny port wine standing in for the heavier stuff. The verdict: still totally delicious.

¼ ounce simple syrup (see recipe below)	¾ ounce cream
1 ½ ounces brandy	1 egg yolk
¼ ounce tawny port	nutmeg
3½ ounces milk	

1. Make the simple syrup by heating 1 part water with 1 part sugar in a saucepan until boiling. Lower the heat and stir constantly until the sugar dissolves.
2. Combine all ingredients except nutmeg with crushed ice in a cocktail shaker or blender.
3. Blend until cold and thoroughly combined.
4. Strain into chilled shot glasses.
5. Sprinkle nutmeg over each shot and serve.

Tip: If you're blending eggnog in a cocktail shaker rather than an electric blender, be sure to shake that thing vigorously so the egg combines completely into the drink. Think of it as a little pre-party warm-up exercise.

STATS: Difficulty: 1   Potency: 1   Garnish: nutmeg

Traditional Eggnog

Serves 32

If you don't have a well-worn recipe already, give this classic rum-and-brandy version a shot.

6 eggs
½ teaspoon vanilla extract
¼ teaspoon ground nutmeg
1 cup plus 1 tablespoon sugar
¾ cup brandy

⅓ cup dark rum
2 cups whipping cream
2 cups milk
ground nutmeg

1. Beat the eggs with an electric mixer on medium for 2–3 minutes, or until frothy.

2. Gradually beat in the vanilla, nutmeg, and sugar. Turn off the mixer.

3. Stir in the brandy, rum, whipping cream, and milk.

4. Refrigerate until ready to serve.

5. Pour into shot glasses.

6. Sprinkle nutmeg over each shot for a spicy garnish.

STATS: Difficulty: 1   Potency: 1   Garnish: nutmeg

Coffee Eggnog

Serves 5

Whisky and coffee add an eye-opening jolt to this eggnog recipe. A perfect drink to either start or end a party with, it will ensure your guests stay awake.

1 teaspoon simple syrup (see recipe below)
2 ounces Scotch whisky
1 ounce Kahlua
6 ounces milk

1 ounce half-and-half
½ teaspoon instant coffee
1 egg
cinnamon

1. Make the simple syrup by heating 1 part water with 1 part sugar in a saucepan until boiling. Lower the heat and stir constantly until the sugar dissolves.

2. Combine all ingredients except cinnamon with crushed ice in a blender.

3. Blend until thoroughly combined.

4. Strain into chilled shot glasses.

5. Sprinkle cinnamon over each shot and serve.

STATS: Difficulty: 1   Potency: 1   Garnish: cinnamon

Baltimore Eggnog

Serves 60

Rich, creamy, and potent, Baltimore Eggnog originally appeared in a local cookbook in 1945. Peach brandy adds a sweet, fruity touch to your standard 'nog repertoire, but feel free to experiment with spiced, pear, apple, or apricot brandies for different flavors. This is clearly a large batch so feel free to cut the recipe in half if you're not so popular, or dole these out in larger servings.

12 eggs
2 cups superfine sugar or confectioner's sugar
1 pint cognac
1 cup dark rum

1 cup peach brandy or Madeira wine
3 pints milk
1 pint cream
grated nutmeg

1. Separate the eggs and beat the yolks with sugar until consistency is thick.

2. Slowly stir in the cognac, rum, peach brandy (or Madeira wine), milk, and cream.

3. Refrigerate until thoroughly chilled.

4. In a separate bowl, beat the egg whites until they are stiff.

5. When the eggnog is ready to serve, pour the egg-yolk mixture into a chilled punch bowl with no ice.

6. Fold in the egg whites; do not beat or stir.

7. Place grated nutmeg near the bowl so guests can garnish their shots as desired.

STATS: Difficulty: 3   Potency: 2   Garnish: nutmeg

Christmas Cheer

With a peppermint twist on this holiday staple, Christmas Cheer will be deliciously (and thankfully) plentiful.

½ ounce eggnog (see Traditional Eggnog on page 112)
½ ounce peppermint schnapps

1. Combine the eggnog and schnapps with crushed ice in a cocktail shaker.

2. Shake until cold and well blended.

3. Strain into a shot glass, and bottoms up!

STATS: Difficulty: 1   Potency: 2

Boost Your Booze IQ

At one point only available to the wealthiest classes of Great Britain, early eggnog incarnations typically contained brandy or Madeira in the milk-and-egg mix. During the 1700s, the beverage took off in America as a rum-based cocktail, with rum made available and more affordable through trade routes in the Caribbean. Over time, Americans began swapping out the rum for whiskey and bourbon, broadening the eggnog menu to suit varieties of tastes and wallets.

General Harrison's Eggnog

Serves 4

William Henry Harrison: revered military hero, president of the United States... booze buff? It's true. "Old Tippacanoe" loved to drink, and during his 1840 presidential campaign he became famous for his boozy pursuits. This eggnog recipe was one of his favorites. Rather than brandy, rum, and cream, it calls for hard cider, giving it a crisper taste and lighter body than traditional eggnogs.

1 teaspoon simple syrup (see recipe below)	nutmeg
1 egg	maraschino cherry
1 cup hard cider	

1. Make the simple syrup by heating 1 part water with 1 part sugar in a saucepan until boiling. Lower the heat and stir constantly until the sugar dissolves.

2. Combine all ingredients with crushed ice in a blender.

3. Blend until cold and well combined.

4. Pour into individual shot glasses.

5. Sprinkle each shot with nutmeg, and add a stemless cherry for garnish if desired.

6. Salute the flag and knock it back.

Variation: For a non-alcoholic version, trade the hard cider for plain ol' regular cider.

STATS: **Difficulty:** 1 **Potency:** 1 **Garnish:** nutmeg, maraschino cherry

Chapter 6

Jell-O Shots

Okay, seriously, who doesn't love a Jell-O shot? And these aren't your run-of-the-mill, one-flavor, boring ol' Jell-O shots. These are gourmet and layered concoctions that will impress everyone within a fifty-foot radius. We've got red-and-white-striped Kandy Kane Jell-O Shots, Jell-O Gingerbread Men, and Christmas Cookie Jell-O Shots. Want to make something red and green? Try Merry Happy Jolly Jell-O Shots. Plus, we've even got a blue and white stunner for those of you who celebrate Hanukkah (Hannukah Sparkler). While these shots may be more time-consuming, the rewards will be that much greater, we promise.

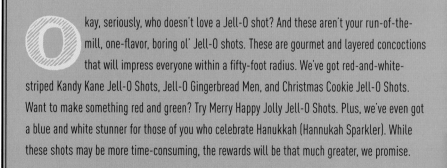

Christmas Cookie Jell-O Shots

Serves 10

Why leave boring cookies and milk for Santa when you can wow him with these delicious cookie-flavored Jell-O shots with a kick? And, you can have lots of fun decorating them with sprinkles, colored sugars, or whatever else you find in the cake-decorating section of your grocery store.

2 cups boiling water
4 envelopes unflavored gelatin
1 cup Bailey's Irish Cream, chilled
½ cup butterscotch liqueur, chilled

¼ cup Cointreau, chilled
¼ cup cold water
whipped cream
sprinkles or other decorations

1. In a large bowl, add the boiling water to the gelatin and stir until completely dissolved.

2. Stir in the Bailey's, butterscotch liqueur, Cointreau, and cold water.

3. Pour the mixture into small cups, leaving room to add whipped cream later.

4. Refrigerate for about 4 hours, or until set.

5. Add some whipped cream to the top of each Jell-O cup.

6. Decorate with sprinkles and watch the smiles spread.

STATS: **Difficulty:** 2 **Potency:** 1 **Garnish:** whipped cream, sprinkles

Kandy Kane Jell-O Shots

Serves 30

'Tis the season for candy canes, but why settle for boring ol' normal candy canes when you can makes these yummy and beautiful candy-cane-flavored Jell-O shots? Try not to be intimidated by the multiple steps—they're really pretty easy!

Red Layer

1 cup boiling water
2 packets cherry Jell-O

½ cup vodka
½ cup cinnamon schnapps

White Layer

1 can sweetened condensed milk
1 cup boiling water
2 envelopes unflavored gelatin

½ cup cold water
¾ cup peppermint schnapps

Garnish

whipped cream
2 candy canes, crushed

1. For the red layer: In a large bowl, add the boiling water to the cherry Jell-O and stir until the Jell-O is dissolved.

2. Let cool to room temperature.

3. Add the vodka and cinnamon schnapps and stir to combine. *(continued on next page)*

4. Set aside.

5. For the white layer: In a large bowl, mix the sweetened condensed milk with ½ cup boiling water.

6. In a small bowl, sprinkle the unflavored gelatin over ½ cup cold water.

7. Let stand a few minutes and then add ½ cup boiling water to dissolve the gelatin.

8. Add the gelatin to the milk mixture and stir to combine.

9. Let cool to room temperature.

10. Add the peppermint schnapps and stir until combined.

11. To make alternating red and white layers, begin by pouring a thin red layer (about 1 inch thick) into small cups.

12. Let this layer set in the refrigerator for about 1 hour or until firm.

13. Pour a thin white layer (about 1 inch thick) on top of the red layer.

14. Let this layer set in the refrigerator for about 1 hour or until firm.

15. Repeat steps 11–14, and you will have four alternating red and white layers. Ta-da!

16. Once they are fully set, decorate with whipped cream and crushed candy cane.

17. Enjoy your beautiful creation.

Variation: You can replace the cherry Jell-O with cranberry-raspberry for a bit of a different flavor.

STATS:

Christmas-Colorful   **Difficulty:** 3
Potency: 2   **Garnish:** whipped cream,
                                    candy cane

How to Slurp Your Jell-O Shot Like a Pro

If you're serving your Jell-O shots in little cups, it may be difficult for your guests to shoot them down—the shot does not easily come out of the cup as the Jell-O has been molded to it and will stick to the sides. How to solve this dilemma? You have a few options:

- Provide little spoons to your guests so they can spoon out the shot.

- Before the party, use a knife to cut around the edges of each shot so it will slide out easily into awaiting mouths.

- Stick a toothpick in each shot and show your guests how to use it to cut around the sides of the shot, loosening it from the cup so they can toss it back.

- Teach your guests how to use their tongues to loosen the shot by sliding their tongue first around the sides of the cup and then sticking it under the Jell-O and sucking it down. Sexy!

Nutcracker Jell-O Shots

Adapted from a recipe by Ilene Miriam Pastry Studio, New York • Serves 10

We have the regular version of this popular cocktail in the book on page 87, but don't you want to make it in Jell-O form? I thought so. This yummy recipe takes it one step further with drunk cherries—a divine invention if I've ever seen one.

2 cups boiling water	½ cup rum
6-ounce packet pineapple Jell-O	½ cup amaretto
1 cup cold water	drunk cherries (see recipe on next page)

1. In a large bowl, add the boiling water to the Jell-O and stir to combine.

2. Slowly stir in the cold water, rum, and amaretto.

3. Pour the mixture into small cups.

4. Drop one drunk cherry into each cup.

5. Refrigerate for about 4 hours, or until set.

6. Try not to down too many of these—those drunk cherries will get ya!

Drunk Cherries

16-ounce jar stemless maraschino cherries
vodka or rum

1. Pour out ¾ of the juice inside of the cherry jar.

2. Fill the jar up with the vodka or rum just enough to cover the cherries.

3. Let the cherries soak in the jar overnight.

Tip: To make the cherries more potent, let them soak for a few days. To make them less strong, pour out less juice (like only ½ or ¼ of the juice).

STATS: Difficulty: 3   Potency: 2

Merry Happy Jolly Jell-O Shots

Serves 10

Your true Christmas colors will shine when you present these layered beauties at a party. They not only look awesome but they taste delicious too, with cranberry, lime, and peppermint layers that are sure to please any palette. They may be a little time-consuming, but trust us, these boozy treats will ensure a merry happy jolly time for all.

Green Layer

3-ounce packet lime Jell-O
1¼ cup boiling water
¾ vodka

Red Layer

⅔ cup cranberry juice
1 envelope unflavored gelatin
⅓ cup vodka

White Layer

1 can sweetened condensed milk
1 cup boiling water, divided
½ cup cold water

2 envelopes unflavored gelatin
¾ cup peppermint schnapps

1. For the green layer: In a large bowl, add the boiling water to the Jell-O and stir until the Jell-O is dissolved.

2. Remove the mixture from heat and let cool to room temperature.

3. Stir in the vodka.

4. Pour the mixture into small cups and refrigerate while preparing the other layers.

5. For the red layer: Pour the cranberry juice into a small saucepan, sprinkle the gelatin on top, and let sit 3 minutes.

6. Heat the mixture and stir until gelatin is dissolved.

7. Remove the mixture from heat and let cool to room temperature.

8. Stir in the vodka.

9. Once the green layer is set (usually about 2 hours), pour the red layer on top and refrigerate until this layer is set (another 2 hours)

10. For the white layer: Mix the sweetened condensed milk with ½ cup boiling water.

11. Pour ½ cup cold water into a small bowl.

12. Sprinkle the gelatin on top.

13. Let it stand a few minutes, then add the remaining ½ cup boiling water and stir to dissolve the gelatin.

14. Add the gelatin mixture to the milk mixture and stir to combine.

15. Cool to room temperature.

16. Pour in the peppermint schnapps.

17. Pour over the set red and green layers and refrigerate until the white layer is set, about 2 hours.

18. Enjoy the "oohs" and "aahs" when you bust these babies out.

Tip: If you have mini candy canes on hand, stick one in each shot for a festive garnish.

Jell-O Gingerbread Men
Serves 10

While these Jell-O shots aren't actually shaped like men, they *do* capture the essence of gingerbread and will remind you of those cute little cookies your mom used to make. Once you taste the alcohol, hopefully you'll forget all about mom.

1 cup sugar
2 cups water, divided
3-inch piece of ginger, peeled and cut into large chunks
2 envelopes unflavored gelatin
2 tablespoons blackstrap molasses
¼ teaspoon cinnamon

¼ teaspoon allspice
dash of nutmeg
½ cup Bailey's Irish Cream
¼ cup butterscotch schnapps
¼ cup cinnamon schnapps
whipped cream

1. Make a ginger simple syrup by heating 1 cup of the water and sugar in a saucepan until the sugar dissolves.

2. Add the ginger to the saucepan.

3. Turn down the heat and simmer a few minutes longer, until the syrup begins to thicken.

4. Remove from heat and let cool.

5. Remove the ginger and strain the syrup into a jar, and set aside.

6. In a saucepan, sprinkle the gelatin over the other cup of water and let sit for a few minutes.

7. Heat over low heat until the gelatin starts to dissolve.

8. Add the molasses, 2 tablespoons of the ginger syrup, and spices.

9. Heat and stir until combined.

10. Remove from heat and let it cool to room temperature.

11. Stir in the Bailey's, butterscotch schnapps, and cinnamon schnapps.

12. Pour into small cups.

13. Refrigerate about 4 hours, or until set.

14. When firm, add whipped cream as a garnish.

15. Savor this alcohol-laced dessert.

Tip: Store your ginger simple syrup in the refrigerator and use it for lots of other drinks, even non-alcoholic ones.

Variation: If you're too lazy to make the ginger simple syrup, you can skip steps 1–5 and substitute ½ teaspoon of ground ginger for the 2 tablespoons of ginger syrup.

STATS: Difficulty: 3   Potency: 1   Garnish: whipped cream

Hanukkah Sparklers

Serves 10

Impress your Jewish friends with these glittering Jell-O shots. Not only do they have shimmery sugar on top, there are even champagne bubbles in the blue Jell-O! These shots are sure to make that dreidel game way more fun.

sugar
1 packet berry blue Jell-O
¾ cup boiling water

¾ cup champagne
¼ cup blue curaçao
¼ cup vodka

1. Coat the rims of the small cups with sugar (for instructions, see page 26).

2. In a medium bowl, stir together the berry blue Jell-O and boiling water until the Jell-O is completely dissolved.

3. Let cool to room temperature.

4. Add the champagne, blue curaçao, and vodka and stir well to combine.

5. Pour the mixture into the small cups.

6. Refrigerate about 4 hours, or until set.

7. Sprinkle more sugar on top for a sparkly effect.

8. Shoot it back and be proud of your blue tongue.

STATS:

Hanukkah-Colorful
Potency: 1

Difficulty: 2
Garnish: sugar

Chapter 7

Flaming Shots

Flaming drinks have become a hot (pun intended!) order in the boozing world, and there's really no better way to amp up a party than lighting things on fire—safely! Whether you're throwing a crazy holiday bash or just an intimate gathering of close chums, adding flames to the festivities is always a thrill. We've got Christmas-appropriate flamers, from the Flaming Hot Buttered Rum to the Flaming Noël to the Cookie Monster, as well as our New Year's Eve Sparkler that is sure to make yours the best party in town. And pretty much any of these is perfect for Hanukkah: The flames will remind you of the burning candles on your menorah. The bright blue spectacles of lighted drinks will garner *oohs* and *aahs* from your guests, and the associated danger of slamming back flaming shots creates an awesome, unique drinking experience. However, that danger is DEADLY serious: Read our Rules for Fire Safety on page 31 before you set *anything* ablaze. (You might want a hot party, but you don't want to singe eyebrows—or worse, seriously burn any guest at your gathering.)

Be responsible and take all fire-safety precautions so you and your pals will have one blazin' holiday celebration.

Flaming Hot Buttered Rum

Serves 12

Hot buttered rum is a smooth, delicious holiday libation for chilly nights. The best way to prepare this winter warmer is by making a large batch of the base mixture and then adding it to rum-filled shot glasses once it's prepared. And then light those babies on fire.

8 ounces (2 sticks) unsalted butter, softened to room temperature and cut into pieces
1 ⅓ cups (packed) brown sugar
1 cup honey
1 teaspoon freshly grated nutmeg
1 teaspoon ground cinnamon
1 tiny pinch of ground cloves

½ ounce dark rum per serving (6 ounces)
boiling water
sugar
½ ounce 151-proof rum per serving (6 ounces)
grated nutmeg

1. Cream the butter, brown sugar, honey, and spices together in a large bowl.

2. Beat the batter until it is fluffy and well blended.

3. Pour the dark rum in ½-ounce portions into shot glasses.

4. Fill the rest of each glass with boiling water, leaving a ¹/₂ inch of room on the top.

5. Top each glass with a dollop of the butter batter.

(continued on next page)

6. Sprinkle a pinch of sugar into each shot glass.

7. Using the back of a spoon, slowly pour a layer of 151-proof rum on top of each shot.

8. Light the rum on fire with a lighter or match.

9. Sprinkle with nutmeg, and enjoy the show.

10. Blow out the flames or place an empty shot glass over each one to extinguish before swallowing this divine drink.

Tip: Don't feel like making all 12 servings at once? The batter mixture will keep in the refrigerator for a few days and in the freezer for a few months. Just pull it out whenever you want a little treat!

STATS:    Difficulty: 3   Potency: 1   Garnish: nutmeg

Reminder: Read our Rules for Fire Safety on page 31 before you set anything ablaze.

Champagne Supernova Bomb

The Supernova is one awesome party drink. First, you see the red and green layers of booze (blue Hpnotiq mixes with the rum to make a festive green). Then, you ignite the shot and marvel at the pretty flame, before dropping this bomb into a sweet glass of champagne. What a way to ring in the New Year!

splash Chambord
¼ ounce Hpnotiq liqueur

¾ ounce 151-proof rum
6–8 ounces Champagne, in a large glass

1. Pour the Chambord into a shot glass.
2. Using the back of a spoon, layer the Hpnotiq on top of the Chambord. Repeat for a layer of 151-proof rum.
3. Light the top on fire with a lighter or match.
4. Admire the fireworks and say a prayer for the new year (and your liver).
5. Drop the flaming shot into a glass of champagne, and chug it down!

STATS: Difficulty: Potency:

Flaming Shot Do's and Don'ts

Don't pour alcohol into an already-lit shot. The flames could blow back and scorch your face.

Don't use more than the indicated amount of your flaming agent (151-proof rum, Everclear, or high-proof whiskey or brandy).

Don't keep open bottles of booze near a flame.

Don't tend a flaming shot bar while drunk.

Don't wear a tie or dangling ribbons or a shirt with loose sleeves or clunky jewelry while preparing flaming drinks.

Don't try to be a badass by chugging the shot while it's on fire—you'll be the biggest dumbass in the ER.

Do keep a large pitcher of water nearby, should a flame get out of hand.

Do use only long matches or skewers or a long campfire lighter to light your drinks.

Do stay on your toes for the duration of the drink-lighting (in other words, don't get sloshed until the fireworks are over).

Do assign a responsible, sober buddy with fire marshal duties.

Do have a stinkin' blast. But don't ignite one!

Flaming Noël

Also known as the Flaming Rasta, this recipe calls for multicolored liqueurs that make it a perfect holiday-party shot. But, the red-gold-green scheme also symbolizes elements of Rastafarian culture: grenadine's red is believed to honor the blood of martyrs, crème de menthe's green the landscape of Jamaica, and Irish cream's gold the wealth of Africa. So toss this one back in the name of Santa *and* Rastafari pride.

½ ounce grenadine syrup
½ ounce Bailey's Irish Cream
½ ounce green crème de menthe
splash 151-proof rum

1. Pour the grenadine into a shot glass.

2. Using the back of a spoon, slowly pour a layer of Bailey's over the grenadine.

3. Again using the spoon, repeat for layers of crème de menthe and 151-proof rum.

4. Light the rum on fire with a lighter or match.

5. Place an empty shot glass over the top to extinguish the flame. Bottoms up!

STATS: Christmas-Colorful   **Difficulty:** 3   **Potency:** 2

Cookie Monster

A scrumptious concoction for children of legal age and dubious morals, this cookie-flavored shot is best slurped through a straw—just like a milkshake.

½ ounce Kahlua
½ ounce Bailey's Irish Cream
splash 151-proof rum

1. Pour the Kahlua into a shot glass.

2. Using the back of a spoon, slowly pour a layer of Bailey's on top of the Kahlua.

3. Again using the spoon, pour a layer of the 151-proof rum on top.

4. Light the rum on fire with a lighter or match.

5. Wait a few seconds and savor the sparks. Then blow out the flame, stick a straw in the glass, and drink up.

STATS: Difficulty: 3 Potency: 3

New Year's Eve Sparkler

Sparks fly when you light this party-starting shot, commonly called the Southern Bound Meteor. The Goldschläger and cherry team up to create a super-cool red-and-gold spectacle.

> stemless maraschino cherry
> ½ ounce Southern Comfort
> ½ ounce Goldschläger
> splash 151-proof rum

1. Place the cherry in a tall shot glass.

2. Pour the Southern Comfort into the glass, followed by the Goldschläger.

3. Slowly pour the 151-proof rum on top.

4. Light the top with a lighter or match.

5. Savor the sparkles. Then place an empty shot glass over the top to extinguish the flame and consume.

  Difficulty: 2   **Potency:** 3   **Garnish:** maraschino cherry

Index

About Cider Mill Press Book Publishers

Good ideas ripen with time. From seed to harvest, Cider Mill Press brings
fine reading, information, and entertainment together between the covers
of its creatively crafted books. Our Cider Mill bears fruit twice a year,
publishing a new crop of titles each spring and fall.

Visit us on the Web at
www.cidermillpress.com
or write to us at
12 Port Farm Road
Kennebunkport, Maine 04046